6-Step Guide *to* Planning *a* Fail-Proof Event

Bonita L. Parker
Certified Event Specialist

© Copyright 2014 - Bonita L. Parker, Bonita Parker Enterprises

ISBN- 1499147007
ISBN-13- 978-1499147001

This book is designed to provide accurate and authoritative information on the subject of event planning. While all of the anecdotes and case studies described in the book are based on valuable and real experiences, the information in conclusive to individual need and experiences. It is sold with the understanding that neither the Author nor the Publisher is engaged in rendering professional services by publishing this book.

All rights reserved for entire book. No part of this book may be reproduced or transmitted in any form or by any means, electronic or mechanical, including photocopy, recording or by any information storage and retrieval system, without permission in writing from author.

Your Event Planner in a Box

6-Step Guide *to* Planning *a* Fail-Proof Event

The Event Planning QUEEN

INTRODUCTION

From concept to completion, this quick reference guide provides detailed insight and unique strategies to increase your event planning success. This easy to follow guide includes my own personal systems and analyses to guide you through avoiding general planning mistakes and shows you a ton of ways to save time and money in all major facets of event planning! This fail-proof guide equips the reader with tried and proven tips and creative problem-solving techniques that can be applied to any event of any size - whether it is a launch event, seminar, or multi-day conference - you will look like the professional. In each chapter, you will discover methods to assist with finding your event purpose, mapping out your budget, choosing the perfect location, and narrowing down your target audience. I have also included real-life case studies that you will easily resonate with as they follow the ins and outs of the event planning process. Whether you are a professional planner or a novice, the information provided in this guide will be insightful and relative to planning with confidence and achieving success in all future events!

TABLE OF CONTENTS

Preface..Page 8

6-Step Planning Wheel..Page 9

Defining Your Ideas..Page 10

Defining The Objectives...Page 14

Defining Your Target Audience...............................Page 18

2- Step Target Finder..Page 21

Defining Proper Timing..Page 23

Defining the Perfect Location.................................Page 26

Defining the Budget...Page 29

Implementation Phase..Page 35

Case Study: Meeting and Event Analysis................Page 36

Appendix I...Page 50

Appendix II..Page 51

About the Author...Page 54

PREFACE

Before you jump head first into throwing an event, whether it's a small meeting or a large conference, you need to devise a strategy. *A plan of action.* Strategizing on your event helps to combine all of your thoughts and ideas into a plan of action, and thus will become the most important tool as you delve into the process.

Having planned events for many years for people of all genres, and observing them as they planned their own events, I have paid close attention to the biggest mistakes people make as a result of lack of strategizing. The key to planning a successful event involves doing the leg work and obtaining the right information necessary to devise your strategy. All of this should be included in your plan of action as any missed insight will only hinder your chances for event success.

Be sure to take your time when coming up with your strategy and give yourself enough time for strategic planning. Putting on a successful event is already tedious enough without having the added pressure of a time constraint, right?

My hope with this book is to help guide you in the right direction. This is why I am divulging my own roadmap to event success by providing you with my personal top secret *6 Step Planning Wheel* that I use to create successful events for my clients.

Don't worry - you can thank me later! Now let's move forward.

> "The blueprint for success is inside you. It will stay there unless you take it out and create it."
>
> --Larina Kase

6- STEP PLANNING WHEEL

There are six primary steps in planning an event - *any event*. No matter the nature of your event, the process to getting it done does not change. By following the outline of my 6-step planning wheel, your journey will guide you from inception to completion *successfully* - and without fail. But pay attention - the process goes rather quickly.

EVENT PLANNING BEGINS

- How? — BUDGET
- What? — IDEAS
- Why? — OBJECTIVES
- Who? — AUDIENCE
- When? — TIMING
- Where? — LOCATION

DEFINING YOUR IDEAS

Good ideas make great events ... or do they?

You may not believe this, but when it comes to planning events, *less is more*. It is so easy to get wrapped up in the excitement of planning an event that out of nowhere ideas will start spewing off the top of your head. And while most of them will seem beneficial to your event, in the end, you may find that they were not as good as you thought. This proves very true when planning conferences and seminars ... leave the *fluffy stuff* at the weddings.

Asking yourself these four simple questions, will help you determine the effectiveness of your ideas:

🖉 What is your vision for your event?

- What makes this event different from events others in your industry are doing?

- What can you do to make this event different from others that your target audience have experienced?

- Why should people attend your event - what can you offer that no one else in your industry is offering?

- How do you stand apart from your competition?

Developing ideas and concepts that automatically speak to what your mission is will help you narrow down what you want the event to encompass. Although mimicking someone else's work is said to be the "highest form of flattery", I would stay away from recreating events that others have done. You want to be the trendsetter in your industry - so let others copy what *you* are doing. Sure it's great to obtain inspiration from your competition, but it is just as imperative that you come up with your own **WOW** factor!

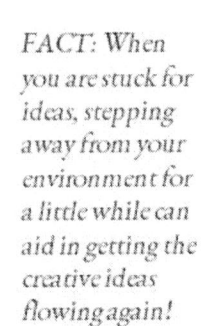

> FACT: When you are stuck for ideas, stepping away from your environment for a little while can aid in getting the creative ideas flowing again!

Even the best event concepts can be wasted if the flow of the event is wrong. For example, lack of foresight could lead you to place a speaker during dinner, rather than before or after a meal. The impact of the speaker is now lost because your guests are too busy paying attention to their food.

Think of your event as a play staged for your audience. There has to be a dramatic development, a constant dynamism across the entirety of the event, in order not to bore your guests. We all know five minutes can either feel like five minutes or it can feel like an hour. The right build-up will keep your audience in suspense until the very last moment.

There are many ways to create a dynamic and engaging event. Event planners learn a lot themselves from watching movies, visiting the theater, and other places of art. As the host of the event, it is key that you understand the basics of generating the right environment for your audience - from incorporating VIP guest seating, the music you may play, the lighting you use and the food you serve. If done well, it will have a lasting impression to your audience; yet if done poorly, it will kill your event flow and risk your reputation for your next event.

Now that we have touched on the WHAT, let's move on to the WHY.

DEFINING THE OBJECTIVES

The single most important question you can ask yourself in this planning process is *why*. Before you start planning, you need to know WHY you are event planning the event in the first place. What is your mission and what are you setting out to accomplish by having this event?

What is funny and slightly pathetic is that I hear so many people saying that the reason they are having an event is "to get some money". My response to that is if that is your sole purpose for having an event, then you have already failed. I say this because after the expenses are paid and the bottom line is dropped, there is no guarantee that you will walk away with any profits. You have to think well beyond the profit margin and devise intangible objectives so as to not overlook all the pertinent details. As the person planning the event, you need to have clear and concise objectives for before, during, and after the event. Now don't get me wrong, I am all for profiting from events, but that should not be the primary goal is all.

Events can be a powerful communication tool for creating lasting memories and customer relationships. They have been deemed a proven way to increase brand awareness, develop new business, and drive business and professional growth. Therefore, asking yourself questions like - what added value is having this event going to produce, or how can this event satisfy growth and marketing goals for my business is a great way to devise those intangible objectives that I spoke on above.

Here are 4 key questions that I ask my clients prior to devising the scope of work for their event. Be sure to utilize them in your own planning objectives:

- Will this event provide new product and service information to potential clients?

- How can this event be formatted to increase brand awareness?

✎ How can this event improve attendance?

✎ How can this event drive sales and increase monetary value?

The event goals stride well beyond answering these questions. Once you obtain clear, attainable goals before the event, measuring its success afterwards is a piece of cake - *not literally* but the planning process will go more smoothly going forward.

Marketing event goals can be broken down into two measures - quantitative and qualitative goals. Here are some examples:

QUANTITATIVE	QUALITATIVE
▪ Introduce New Product	▪ Positive Customer Image
▪ Increase Sales	▪ Positioning above Competitors
▪ Increase Customer Retention	▪ Brand / Product Awareness
▪ Develop Social Media Plan	▪ Positive Customer Attitudes

Based on your event objectives, it's possible to create a general sense of how much it will cost for various elements of your program. This will vary based on the type of event you are hosting, and what it includes.

Many people who organize an event for the first time often fall into the trap of wanting to plan a champagne event on a beer budget. Even though it is possible -- not easy, but possible. That is why many people turn to their event planner for help.

Now that I've assisted you with the WHY aspect of your event, let's move on to the WHO.

DEFINING YOUR TARGET AUDIENCE

You want to invite who? If you are reading this book - you must be an entrepreneur. As an entrepreneur, one of the most common words you will hear on a regular basis is **target market**. What is a target market? By definition, a target market is a specific group of consumers at which a company promotes its products and services. Therefore, after defining your event goals and objectives, you should begin thinking about your target audience. What kind of people will this event attract? Who will attend this event? Who do I want this event to benefit? In order for your event to be successful, you must first know your audience -- who will help you make this event a success.

Starting in business, many entrepreneurs attack it with the belief that their business is going to thrive at a steadfast pace because they have an insurmountable number of family and close friends that are automatically going to lend their support - i.e. dollars. *WRONG!* If you have been in business long enough you have by now realized that your family and friends are more or less the last to support your business. Happy for you - yes ... support - no. Your primary support will come from a unique group of people called *strangers* ... i.e. your target audience.

Define your target audience. Whether you are doing a book signing, launching a new product, or promoting a new service, there is a specific audience awaiting your event. Once you narrow down who these people are, you can have a more concise picture on what is to be expected from your event.

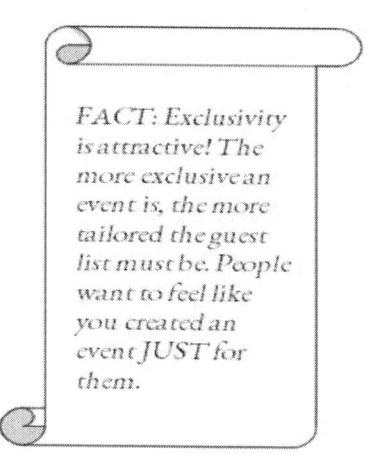

> *FACT: Exclusivity is attractive! The more exclusive an event is, the more tailored the guest list must be. People want to feel like you created an event JUST for them.*

But how do you find these people? Like many entrepreneurs, this is a major source of confusion for you. But not to worry - you are not alone in this. As an event planner, we often have to think quick on our feet to be able to create effective ways of getting your event planned and provide ideas relative to your event - who we think your event will most benefit and why; and what can we do to attract attendees. So I have created my *2-Step Target Finder* comprised of two core questions that are key to finding your target market that I personally use to ensure that the right people are attending my own events.

2-Step Target Finder

Who is actually buying your products now?
Set some time aside to get to know your current clients and customers. Send them a quick survey and ask them things like their age, their gender, where they live, what publications they read, what websites they visit, etc., so you can get to know them better. This will give you an idea of who they are so you know where to find them. Obtaining at least 75-100 responses will give you a good overview of your clients. I've done this once per year with all of my businesses and I've gotten some great insight into who is actually interested in my services. And here's a quick tip: offer your customers something in return for their time (a substantial discount on your services, a free gift, etc.).

Who do you actually enjoy connecting with?
The second thing that comes into play when defining your target market is to look at who you actually enjoy marketing to and connecting with. I knew that one of the audiences that I really love connecting with are brides. I included this group in my target market. When it came time to promote my trade show, the first group of retailers that I reached out to was bridal shops. When it came to pitching my event for publicity, those same shops were at the top of my list. So if there is a specific group of people that you enjoy doing business with, make sure to include them in your target market.

Please note that is it perfectly normal and okay to have more than one **target market**, especially as your business grows, but I always recommend starting out with ONE first and making sure that you completely understand that market before reaching out to others.

Remember, you can't *wow* them if you don't know who they are!

Now that we've discussed the WHO ... don't worry, you are halfway to event planning SUCCESS! Let's push forward to the WHEN.

DEFINING PROPER TIMING

I would be remiss to tell you that there is no right time to do an event, but that would be the most inaccurate piece of information that I could ever provide you with. When it comes to events, *timing is everything!*

Part of developing a successful event is mapping out when it is going to take place and how long will it last. Timing plays a huge role on the planning of your event so you want to make sure that your target audience will be able to be there. You want to ensure that you avoid planning events around the holiday seasons where high travel volume is taking place. Nothing worse than having your out-of-state guests enter into a city that is gridlocked. Another thing you want to consider is conventions and special events that could be going on within your city. Not only will this impact negatively on your event's attendance rate, you will be subject to increased fees and stricter guidelines on venue usage.

A key element that I encourage you to consider and research is other events that your venue of choice may be hosting in close time proximity as your event. This could certainly hinder the effectiveness of your event especially *if* an event being hosted shares in a similar mission as your event. This means that your target audience will more than likely be in attendance and thus putting them in a position where they have to choose between events. *So what's so wrong about that* ... you may be thinking. Unless you want to go back to the drawing board trying to come up with new and innovative ways to make your event outshine their event, then absolutely nothing. But if you are happily content and confident with the event you have thus mapped out, then there could possibly be a chance of conflict and depending on how attractive your packaged event is, you may lose attendees, *i.e.* money out of your pockets.

Do your due diligence. It takes little effort to scope out your competition to make sure that the clouds don't rain on your day. Besides, *you want them to attend your fabulous event* so that they can see what YOU are doing - *remember*.

FACT: Checking out what your competition is planning and reviewing your city's social calendar will increase your chances of having a high attendance rate at your event.

Setting your timing is simple ... ask yourself these 3 simple questions:

- When is the best time for me to host my event? (always schedule it around a time when you are least busy and not swamped. This will allow you to truly give your event the special attention it needs to be successfully executed)

- What is happening in my event city? (as mentioned above, you do not want to plan your event during a time when your city is having another major event - for obvious reasons)

- How long will my event last? (your event should never last longer than necessary - 4 hours max.)

Once these key elements are in place, you are on your way to event success and ready to secure your venue!

DEFINING THE
PERFECT LOCATION

So you have successfully defined your event goals, narrowed down your target audience, got your timing in order - the next thing to accomplish is locking down the perfect venue in the right area. Location! Location! Location!

Just how do I find the best location for my event, you might wonder. The first thing I encourage you to do is give great thought to your venue. The perfect venue will be a direct reflection of the event that you are trying to put on. Think about what you want your event to exude or portray to the attendees - be it elegance, a warm inviting atmosphere, a learning experience, etc. Your venue should reflect that -- or be able to be dressed up to reflect that. Your venue is much more than just the house to host your event. Look at is as a stage for your event -- is the location/area right for the attendees you are targeting; is the area in which your audience is traveling from in close enough proximity to your venue - assess how much travel may be involved for them;

and more importantly, be sure that your location offers everything that you need by weighing the pros and cons prior to making your selection.

In the event that you decide to utilize multiple locations for your event, it is imperative to take into consideration the travel time and distances between each location. Tedious and time consuming, yes; but very crucial for the overall success of your event – and I guarantee you will thank me later for telling you this! When you invite people to your events, this is by far the most important thing that factors into the decision-making process of most attendees. I cannot elaborate enough on the importance of location. Understand that whether you are a planner or the person hosting the event, no one will attend if they feel it is too far or problematic for them to get to. Nobody wants to spend a good portion of their time traveling so keep this in mind.

Amenities are also very important when considering a venue. Although majority of venues provide basic amenities to aid in the success of your event, be sure to inquire about maintenance and upkeep. When was the last time they upgraded the facilities and what improvements did they make. This serves dual purposes. In addition to simply ensuring that you are getting the best for your money, any major upgrades can be used as a selling tool to your attendees! Who wouldn't want to attend an event where the guests will feel somewhat of royalty.

Another element to factor in is entertainment! What else is there for your attendees to do after your event is over? Is your event in a location surrounded by museums, parks, shopping, or fine dining? Majority out of town guests want to tour or enjoy life after 5pm when they visit a new city outside of their hometown. Make sure you have a list of suggestions available for them – chances are they will ask you!

Finally, *visit the venue!* Just because you may have a good relationship with the Sales Manager or you did an event there 5 years ago, does not mean that you know what the venue currently offers. Go see for yourself so that you can assess the space, parameters, atmosphere, and set up options to maximize your number of possible attendees. This would be a great time to inquire about recent events that the venue has hosted so that you gain a better understanding of the location and all that it offers.

The choice is yours ... success or failure? One thing for sure is that you can't put this event on without knowing if you can afford to do so. This next chapter discusses BUDGET ... let's see if you are ready ...

DEFINING THE BUDGET

If you were building a house from scratch or running a marketing campaign for your company, would you attempt to do either without a budget? Whether you're a seasoned pro or new to planning events, keeping an event budget will help you stay organized and keep you from going over budget.

Money matters -- do not be mistaken!

There is no such thing as "enough money" when planning an event. There are so many hidden costs and incidentals to be aware of that many people fail to budget for. Going back to my opening statement, once you determine what your house is going to be made from – concrete, wood, stucco or combinations of all three – you would need to know all of the materials necessary to go from wood to windows and working appliances, right? It doesn't do anyone any good if you build this fabulous house and have run out of money and can no longer afford the stove, the finishing touches and the lights. You've spent all this money and your house is unusable. Or what oftentimes happen is that people miscalculate or fail to devise a budget and when they run out of money, look to a bank to make up the shortfall. *Well planning your event is no different ...*

Not adhering to a budget is a costly downfall that many people make when planning - or should I say *lack of* planning. As a planner, my first question will likely be "what is your budget?" And too often I hear the words *"I don't know."* This is tragic! If you have not set aside at minimum $3000 or have it to spare, don't waste time hosting your event. It's that simple. **Money matters**. And I'm here to let you know that it is okay to hold off on your event until you are financially prepared for the costs associated with it. Otherwise, you will be stuck with a bootleg event on a shoestring budget. Now don't get me wrong - I know what you are thinking ... many people have done events on a shoestring budget before and they turned out *okay*. Very true! But they also could have had the support of a savvy event specialist who knew the art of negotiating; they could have had sponsorship in place; or donors - who donated goods and services in support of the event. That's how shoestring budgets work, but not everyone will be in a position to have those things. And furthermore, who wants an event that's just *okay*...

While your budget may have a major impact on the style of your event, it should not stop you from reaching your event goals. Having budget constraints does not mean you have to cut out on creativity, it simply means that you may have to be a little more innovative when it comes to spreading out your ideas. Great things can be accomplished with a small wallet, you just have to know the ins and outs - and how to make it happen!

There is one simple way to mitigate this:

Create a budget!

It's just that simple ...

By not creating a budget, it is quite impossible to stick to one, right? Creating a budget is far easier than you might believe. In the same manner you have to create and stick to a budget to run your home, doing so for your event is actually the same.

Here are 4 quick and easy steps to guide you through this process:

1. Ask yourself how much you realistically have to spend
2. Create a spreadsheet and make certain to subtract as you go
3. Give it the same equal importance you would balancing your checkbook
4. Assume you are not receiving any financial help from outside resources and work with the numbers that YOU actually have on hand

Assessing your own personal financial situation will indeed help you keep control over your budget and always stay abreast of all costs associated with your event. Be sure to obtain accurate quotes from all of your vendors so that as you plug them into your spreadsheet, you will have a better idea of what you will be spending.

TRACK! TRACK! TRACK!

Once you know what you can afford to spend, you have to make sure that you are holding accountable every penny that is deducted from your budget. You can do this by keeping a simple Excel spreadsheet or an event management system such as Planning Pod - an all inclusive tool for event planning. See Appendix 1 for a sample *Budget Spreadsheet*.

Should you notice that your budget is too small, there are ways to make it seem bigger or stretch a little further. This is where sponsorship comes into play and can make a major difference in your event. In brief, sponsors can aid in so many different ways - monetarily, advertising, products and merchandise contributions, printing, etc. *The list goes on and on!* A key element to remember with sponsorship is that anything donated, is considered money in your pocket and an added bonus to your slim budget. To get more insight on how to obtain sponsorship for your events, inquire about my *Sponsorship Basics 101* course to help guide you through the process successfully. Also, please see Appendix 2 for a sample *Sponsorship Solicitation Letter*.

Additionally, well beyond what you aimed to spend, there are several ways to save money and make your budget work for you. Some vital tips are listed below:

NEGOTIATE!

One thing a lot of people do not realize it that no price is set in stone when it comes to booking your venue. The venue is more than likely your biggest ticket price when planning your event. Never accept the fee that the venue gives you - its negotiable! The oldest trick in the book to getting the fee you want is by saying this simple statement: "I'm looking for a home location to host all of my events" and from that point, you will have them eating out of your hands. All venues will work with you if they believe their books will be filled for the year with your events. The idea of repeat business is how they make their money. So set your price and state those words and see what happens! Its works for me ALL the time. – :)

REDUCE!

The size of your event often plays a major role in how much you will spend on your event. Be it food and beverage costs per person, gift bags, marketing materials, or even the set up required, this is money charged or being spent out of your pockets. Reducing the size of your event will also reduce costs! This also applies to improvising on your theme. Perhaps your budget does not allow you to have diamonds and pearls but you can use crystals and oyster shells to accomplish the same look.

OUTSOURCE!

This is by far your best option next to obtaining sponsors for your event. Outsource the costs of your event to local entrepreneurs looking for the opportunity to promote their products and services! Vendors are the key to making sure that some of the event fees are covered by someone other than yourself. Money derived from selling vendor tables at your event can be used to cover the bulk of if not all the costs if the price points are strategically set. So if you are working with a tight budget, this is a great way to expand those numbers a bit!

IMPLEMENTATION PHASE

Now that you have test drove all of the major steps required to planning a fail proof event, it is time to implement everything that you've just learned in the previous chapters of this guide.

Whether this is your first event or you've planned many others, a thing to keep in mind is that you achieve event success, you must stick to the strategy and follow the steps. Now, let the planning begin!

CASE STUDY: MEETING & EVENT ANALYSIS

All the planning and preparation in the world cannot stop nature from happening and affecting the outcome of your events. Couple that with a client who is determined to go full speed ahead with planning their event, against all odds, and overcome the adversaries.

The following case studies are designed to provide an outlook into the event planning industry from a novice perspective. The following entrepreneurs have been interviewed regarding their personalized experiences with planning and hosting private events without the use of an experienced event specialist.

These personal experiences are not designed to deter you from self-planning, but rather provide insight on the challenges and obstacles one may face without incorporating guidelines and obtaining insight from planner mentors.

So how do you make the best of a bad situation? This case study offers some advice.

Question:

How important do you believe incorporating themes and unique ideas are in your events? Does it really make a difference in the outcome of the event to have one - why or why not?

Analysis

I think themes and unique ideas are significant. Being unique will set you apart from your competitors. It also adds flair of creativity that will make the event a social mouth piece well after the event. Themes and unique ideas will set you up to dominate your sphere...the more unique the better.

Conclusions and Recommendations

Great ideas make great events! But be careful to not overdo it. Sometimes going over-the-top in your ideas only work well for circuses, and you want your event to be a reflection of who you are and what your event will represent.

Utilize the incredible tips and the *4 Effective Questions* when developing ideas for your event. This will certainly keep you on track and within the realm of creativity.

Details of this case study were provided by Nisha Parker, CEO of Synergy, an Empowerment Organization. All conclusions and recommendations were written by author. For more information on Nisha Parker, please visit www.synergylounge.org

Defining Your Event Objectives

Question:

In your experience planning events, when it comes to defining the objective of your event, what was the biggest obstacle that you encompassed when determining your "WHY"? Provide history of the event and how you came to your decision to do the event.

Analysis

The objective for any Synergy event has always been driven by my mission – which is to empower people in their endeavors to reach their potential, and in turn, to encourage them to help the global community to become a better place by volunteering and giving back.

The challenge for me has been in selecting a topic to focus on considering the broad spectrum of empowerment activities, i.e. relationships, youth, etc. I've learned to go with the flow by becoming conscious of the desires people communicate during my coaching sessions or in ordinary conversations. If you listen, people will tell you want they want –just flow with it.

Conclusions and Recommendations

If you revert back to the chapter on *Defining your Objectives*, this is a clear example of how doing your research and implementing a clear and concise objective will allow you to overcome the adversary of narrowing down your event to focus on one particular objective - one that will drive your target audience your way.

Utilizing my personal *4-key questions* technique that I ask my clients when helping them develop a precise scope of work and planning objective for their event will assist you a great deal if this is an area that you struggle with.

Details of this case study was provided by Nisha Parker, CEO of Synergy, an Empowerment Organization. All conclusions and recommendations were written by author. For more information on Nisha Parker, please visit www.synergylounge.org

Defining Your Target Audience

Question:

What in your opinion are the biggest hurdles people face when trying to niche down the target audience for their event? What steps do you encourage people to undergo when trying to determine the correct audience to buy into products and services?

Analysis

There is much value in determining a niche market. Narrowing down my niche was very difficult when I first pursued business...I attribute this to my desire to want to empower people – everybody, not just a segment of society. In my communication with peers, I have found this to be the common thread, particularly for empowerment organizations. However, it is very important for aspiring business owners to explore and determine their audience early on. It saves time, money and other resources that could otherwise go to research and marketing efforts.

As a coach, I encourage entrepreneurs to conduct statistical research on the primary consumers of their products and services. This information is readily available via Google and trade association publications. The more research you conduct, the better equipped you are to make informed decisions on where to direct your financial efforts. If done properly, this ultimately will lead to increased product sales, increase your competitive edge, and ultimately put you on the path to dominate your sphere.

Conclusions and Recommendations

In reviewing the chapter on *Defining Your Target Audience*, it speaks to this very situation in a direct way. What is clearly demonstrated is an individual who did the legwork to find out who would best benefit from the services she was providing. Great success comes to those who work hard towards it!

Finding your target market is no easy fiat. This is why taking advantage of my *2-Step Target Finder* makes this process less painful - it's quick and easy, and quite successful.

Details of this case study was provided by Nisha Parker, CEO of Synergy, an Empowerment Organization. All conclusions and recommendations were written by author. For more information on Nisha Parker, please visit www.synergylounge.org

Defining Timing

Analysis

When I first started out, I did not consider the significance of timing. I quickly learned to explore competing events, particularly ones that were in the same geographic location where I proposed to have my event. In 2008, I held a youth empowerment event, and quickly learned that most school aged children were on vacation in August. Luckily this was a quick fix—I switched future youth events to school season to increase the attendance.

I also learned to tap into special holidays or national events to piggyback upon for my events. For example, Valentine's Day is the ideal time to have a "relationship seminar for singles". Perfect timing can enhance the success of your event.

Conclusions and Recommendations

As it relates to timing, this chapter reiterates as key element that the writer mentions above, *"Perfect timing can enhance the success of your event."* I was extremely glad to read that the writer quickly learned that timing was equivalent to success - although the hard way. Imagine if she did not have that insight to learn from what could have been a very costly mistake. It takes but only a few minutes to do research to see what is happening in your city and surrounding areas that may have an effect on your event.

Take advantage of my 3 simple questions provided at the end of the chapter entitled, *"Defining Proper Timing."*

Details of this case study was provided by Nisha Parker, CEO of Synergy, an Empowerment Organization. All conclusions and recommendations were written by author. For more information on Nisha Parker, please visit www.synergylounge.org

Defining the Perfect Location

Question-

As a professional speaker, it is common that location / venue choice can inadvertently affect your image while you are on stage engaging the audience. What are your views on that statement and what would you recommend as an effective guideline to incorporate into the planning process as it relates to speakers?

Analysis

Speakers are aesthetic by nature –so the venue appearance is very important. It also speaks volumes about your brand.

My recommendation for event planners, business owners, etc. is to visit the venue to make sure it's consistent with your brand. The décor, cleanliness, interior design, civility of wait staff, etc. should be inspected before you advertise the event. The surrounding area is another element that must be explored. For example, traffic, parking, cleanliness in the external areas, congregating of employees outside, etc.

All of these things can make a good or bad impression on your brand –make sure you check the venue out completely before you book it.

Conclusions and Recommendations

In reiteration, venue appearance is very important to your business brand. One thing that I can attest to as a planner, but more importantly as someone who often is in the presence of others who attend certain events is that people are critical. Your personal brand will be quickly diminished if your venue is all wrong. Do not make the mistake of not thoroughly inspecting your venue of choice.

Please revert back to my chapter on *"Defining the Perfect Location"* to read more in depth on guidelines to follow and look for when choosing the perfect location.

Details of this case study was provided by Nisha Parker, CEO of Synergy, an Empowerment Organization. All conclusions and recommendations were written by author. For more information on Nisha Parker, please visit www.synergylounge.org

Defining Your Budget

Question-

Discuss the importance of proper budgeting for an event. What, if any, was your biggest obstacle regarding budgeting or lack of advanced budget planning?

Analysis

A budget provides the financial boundaries for the event. It guides your decision and keeps you on track to estimate the desired revenue for the event.

My most significant mistake during the early stages of my entrepreneur career was not developing a budget. This caused me to overspend, and I believe it minimized my ability to obtain the desired revenue. I was constantly adding new items and paying way too much. A firm budget would have set the footprint and constrained my spending to necessities not wants.

Conclusions and Recommendations

"Defining the Budget" .... I cannot stress enough the importance of making your money matter. As you read above, not defining your budget is a very costly downfall that many people make during the planning of their events. As the writer pointed out, overspending and not reaching revenue heights was a major error for her in the planning process. Do not let the mistake of many, be *your* mistake as well.

Implementing my *4 quick and easy steps* to developing your budget will help save you not only time and money, but will increase the opportunity for a satisfactory revenue outcome.

Details of this case study was provided by Nisha Parker, CEO of Synergy, an Empowerment Organization. All conclusions and recommendations were written by author. For more information on Nisha Parker, please visit www.synergylounge.org

APPENDIX 1: KEY ELEMENTS TO DEVISING YOUR EVENT BUDGET

When devising your event budget, use this sample budget spreadsheet:

ITEM	PROJECTED (anticipated costs)	ACTUAL (actual costs)	DETAILS
Venue			
Catering (include tips and gratuities)			
Transportation (include shuttles, transfers, limo)			
Decor (include centerpieces, florals, rentals, etc.)			
Entertainment (honorariums)			
Equipment (include A/V, rented furniture)			
Printing			
Advertising			
Supplies			
Gifts / Gift bags			
Speakers			
Audio Visual			
Other / Misc.			
Contingencies			

APPENDIX 2: SPONSOR SOLICITATION LETTER

Title
Company
Address
City, State, Zip

Dear Sponsor Contact:

I am contacting you regarding a unique sponsorship opportunity for (Company).

On (date), (Company) of (location) will host a (type of event) featuring (keynote name, title, company). This event, titled (title of event), will attract (number of attendees / target audience) from the (city of event) community.

Last year, (event title) drew 225 attendees and the participation of 15 well-known commercial accessory designers. It was cosponsored by (name of previous sponsor) and marketed as a networking event for business and professional women in the downtown area. The event drew an affluent audience – average household income was $130,000. Some 30 percent of the attendees purchased products from the event. (this section is designed to give specs on the previous year / most recent event of its kind)

We invite (Company) to be the exclusive (type of sponsor) represented at (event title) for (year). In addition to being listed on all advertising and press as a sponsor of the event, (Company) will have the opportunity to host a booth at the event to display products.

Sponsorship benefits such as promotional coupons in all goodie bags included the raffle may be used to drive traffic to (Company) after the event. (Be sure to provide as many CORE sponsor benefits as possible in this section)

We hope to have the opportunity to share our full presentation of sponsorship benefits with you in the near future.

I will contact you on (date, time) to determine if a meeting is warranted. In the meantime, please do not hesitate to contact me at (phone number/email) with any questions.

Sincerely,

Name
Event Coordinator

ABOUT THE AUTHOR

Bonita Parker, Owner and Sr. Event Specialist of *BMS Event Management Group* is a Maryland native. While working full-time in corporate America, she achieved her degree in Business and encompasses extensive business management and marketing insight, as well as over 14 years of experience planning and coordinating corporate conferences and seminars, and a multitude of social events that range from weddings to milestone birthday parties.

Her personality is harmonious with the organizational demands of an Events Specialist. As a hobby, she familiarized herself with the ins and outs of event planning by aligning herself with skillful mentors and keeping up with the latest event trends. Melding her corporate background with her entrepreneurial mindset, Bonita successfully manages the day-to-day operations of *BMS Event Management Group*, as well as oversee the development of her individual company, *Bonita Parker Enterprises*.

A huge advocate for individuals turning their passions and favorite pastimes into a successful career, Bonita incorporated her own education with her years of experience, and devised a 6-week accelerated coaching program where she mentors individuals on the ins and outs of starting your own event planning business and incorporating *proven* business-building strategies that will generate increased clientele and business success.

Her most recent successes included planning and hosting several trade shows and social events that housed known-named individuals like all-American actress *Tasha Smith*, best known for her role in Tyler Perry's *"Why Did I Get Married"*, business guru *Stedman Graham*; *Jennifer*

Williams of VH1's hit reality TV show *"Basketball Wives"*; R&B songstress *Chante Moore*; ABC's Secret Millionaire *James Malinchak*; and *Lasse Larsen* of VH1's hit reality show *"What Chili Wants"*. She has also planned and coordinated a multitude of corporate seminars and conferences for companies such as Vicki Irvin Enterprises – a multimillion dollar coaching practice operated by business coach and nationally-known speaker, *Vicki Irvin* and overseeing multi-day bi-annual conferences for internet marketer and UFC mixed martial arts trainer *Master Lloyd Irvin, Jr.* of Lloyd Irvin Mixed Martial Arts Academy.

Because of her niche` for negotiating price points and saving her clients thousands of dollars on each event, she has become one of the most sought-after event specialists in her area and has been dubbed *The Event Planning Queen* by many who have used her services.

Strategy Courses
- *"Event Planning 101 – From Inception to Completion"*
- *"Sponsorship Basics 101 - 5-Call Tele-series"*

Other Resources
- *"The Ultimate Event Planning Toolkit"* (coming soon)
- *"Your Event Planner in a Box: 6- Step Guide to Planning a Fail-Proof Event"*

- "Success in Sponsorship: 10-Step Guide to Achieving Corporate Sponsors" e-Book
-"10 Simple Steps to Overcoming Your Event Planning Oopsies" e-Book
-"The Ultimate Event Planner – Your Guide to Full Service Event Planning"

Made in the USA
Charleston, SC
10 May 2014